Iguazu Falls from the Brazilian side
Iguazú Falls from the International Space Station, 2016
BRAZIL
Iguazú River
Gorge
Hotels
Hotels
Devil's Throat
Spray
N
ARGE

Iguazu Falls Cataracts Brazil Nature
Iguazu Falls Cataracts Brazil Nature

Iguazu Cascade Falls Waterfall Brazil
Iguazú Waterfalls Waterfall Water Wall Iguazu Water

Tucano Bird Brazil Nature Cataracts Ride
Ticket Office - Iguaçu National Park, Brazil

Iguazu Iguacu Iguasu Falls Waterfall South
Ecological Train to Devil's Throat, Iguazu National Park, Argentina.

Iguazu Falls Cataracts Brazil Nature
Cataract Iguaçú Waterfall Iguazu Falls Brazil

Scenery Iguazu Falls Argentina South America

Iguazu Brazil
Waterfall Brazil Iguazu Cataratas De Iguazu

Cascade Nature Travel Iguazu Brazilwood
Heron Birds Iguazu Nature Bird Waterfalls

Brazil Iguazu Iguazu Waterfalls Waterfall Nature
Iguassu Brazil Waterfall Nature Spray Argentina

Waterfall Falls River Natural Cascade Scenic
Iguassu Brazil Waterfall Nature Spray Argentina

Iguazu Waterfall Landscape Tourism Brazil
Iguassu Brazil Waterfall Nature Spray Argentina

Devil's Throat. View From Iguazu National Park, Argentina.
Iguazu Waterfall-Argentina Falls Flow Landscape

Iguassu Brazil Waterfall Nature Spray Argentina

Waterfall Falls Water Murky Scenic Forest
Flowing

Iguazu Nature Birds
Runway Iguazú Falls Argentina Astounding Cascades

Waterfall Churning Tumultuous Mist Rough
Water
Reptile Lizard Animal Argentina Argentinian Fauna

Tiger Ant Ant Insect Black Ant Big Ant
Iguazu Waterfall Argentina Falls Flow Landscape

Argentina Brazil Iguazu Iguacu Falls River
Iguazu Brazil Wass Force Of Nature

Iguazu Waterfall Cascade Brazil National Park
Falls Iguazu Sunset Brazil

Argentina Iguazu Waterfall River Landscape
Iguazu Falls Iguazu Waterfall South America Travel

Falls Iguazu Landscape Water Brazil Fall
Falls Nature Water Current Fall Waterfalls Height

Foz Do Iguaçu Water Cataracts Brazil Nature Paraná
Iguazu Falls Natural Body Of Water Landscape Nature

Water Nature Iguazu Landscape Cascade Falls
Iguazu Waterfall Brazil

Iguazu Falls South America Iguazu Water Waterfall
Iguazu River Falls Argentina Tropical Travel

Argentina Iguazu Rainbow Waterfall
Iguazu Falls Waterfalls Brasil Water South America

Waterfall Iguazu Iguaçu The Falls Water Landscape
Brazil Waterfalls Iguazu National Park

Brazil Waterfalls Iguazu National Park
Iguazu Brazil Falls Nature America Travel

Brazil Waterfalls Iguazu National Park
Brazil Waterfalls Iguazu National Park

Iguazu Falls South America Iguazu Waterfall
Brasil Waterfall Brazil Jungle Nature Landscape

Tucano Brazil Bird Forest Zoo Large Spout Animals
Brazil Argentina Iguacu Falls Majestic

Iguazu Waterfall Falls Landscape Brazil
Iguazu Waterfalls River

Iguassu Brazil Waterfall Nature Spray Argentina
Iguazu Waterfall Falls Water Nature Landscape

Iguazu Cascade Falls Landscape
Iguazu Waterfall Iguazu Waterfalls Argentina Water

Iguazu Falls Falls Rainbow Nature Argentina
Brazil Iguazu Waterfall Iguazu National Park

Iguazu Falls Waterfalls Brasil Water South America
Waterfalls Waterfall Foz Do Iguaçu Nature Forest

Foz Iguaçu Cataract Water Foz Do Iguaçu Tourism
Waterfall Brazil Iguaçu Iguazú Waterfalls

Iguazu Waterfall Iguazú Waterfalls Nature Water
Falls Iguazu Iguaccu Cataratas-Water Fall River

Waterfall Cascade Falls River Iguazu Fall
Iguazu Falls Brazil Tour Viewpoint People

Cataracts Water Falls Iguaçu Foz Foz Do Iguaçu
Cataracts Foz Water Falls Waterfall Iguaçu

Iguazu Iguacu Falls Waterfall Butterfly Brazil
Iguazu Falls Water Nature Current Cascade Falls

Iguazu Waterfall Brazil Nature Falls Argentina
Brazil Nature Water Park Iguazu South America

Falls Landscape Water Nature Iguazu Vegetation
River Cataract Water Niagara River Niagara
Canada

Iguazu Falls Water Paraná The Iguaçu River
South America Waterfall Waterfalls Foz De Iguazu

Mouth Iguaçu Iguazu Falls Paraná Trip Tourism
Iguazu Falls Brazil Paraná The Iguaçu River

Cataracts Foz Water Falls Waterfall Iguaçu
Iguassu Brazil Waterfall Nature Spray Argentina

Iguazu Falls Waterfalls Brasil Water South America
Waterfall Cascade Falls Iguazu

Waterfall Iguazu Elements Nature
Iguazu Nature Falls Waterfalls Boat Excursion
Santo de Iguazu

Waterfall Iguazú Argentina
Boat Iguazú Falls Argentina Astounding
Cascades

Falls Iguazu Water Jungle Argentina Landscape
Iguazu Falls Waterfalls Brasil Water South America

Iguazu Waterfall Argentina Water
Nature Vegetation Water Iguazu Falls Argentina

Iguazu Nature Falls Waterfalls
Runway Iguazu Falls Waterfalls Brasil Water South

Argentina Butterfly Insects Beauty
Foz De Iguaçu Cataracts Nature Landscape

Proof